Bygone Gravesend -Vo

COMPILED FROM THE COLLECTION OF MALCOLM JOHN

JOHN HALLEWELL PUBLICATIONS
172 HIGH STREET,
ROCHESTER, KENT.

ISBN 0 905540 25 5

Bygone Series (Kent)

Already available: Bygone Medway (Volumes one to three)
In preparation: Maidstone, Swale, Thanet, Channel Coastlands, Canterbury, Wealden District, Tunbridge Wells, Bygone Craft of Thames and Medway, Bygone Transport of Kent.

Gravesend

Gravesend is the Kentish gateway to the Thames Estuary. Here we have rounded the marshy peninsula of 'Bygone Medway' and head inland for the Pool of London. It is from here that the pilots commence their river journey past the industrial areas of Northfleet and Dartford and on to the relaxing vista of Greenwich.

Pictured three years after the opening of the King Street branch of the London and County Bank (National Westminster). This bank opened its doors originally in 1837 at 17 High Street under the name of Surrey, Kent and Sussex Banking Company. The first move was to 16 High Street after the fire of 1850 and then onto 24 High Street (next to the Old Town Hall) in 1864. King Street Corner was the site of St. Thomas's Almshouses, remaining standing until 1896.

The Clock Tower was erected to commemorate the Golden Jubilee of Queen Victoria in 1887, the cost was just over £1,000 and the architect was John Johnson. It took two years to complete the construction, the foundation stone being laid on 10th September 1887 and work ending on 9th November, 1889. The Chimes were added later in February, 1890.

Trams were planned between Gravesend and Northfleet in 1880. They ran from Milton Road, Brunswick Road, through the town centre to London Road, Northfleet. Originally known as the Gravesend, Rosherville and Northfleet Tramways Co. Ltd, they became electrified in 1890 as the Gravesend and Northfleet Electric Tramway. Maidstone and District replaced them with motor buses in the late 20's.

The Pier erected in 1842 was frequented by the Royal Family as well as day trippers on paddle steamers. The construction caused concern to the lightermen who feared for their livelihoods. Indeed in an interesting broadside petition one can see that they campaigned for the Terrace Pier to be a Waterman's Pier, depriving the sharks and packet owners of their 'easy money'.

This splendid shot shows the transom of a sailing barge beached close to the Royal Terrace Pier. Barges were an integral part of the river front at Gravesend as they plied their route up and down river, gracefully moving on the tide, graceful yet hard work for the crew as described in '*Sailorman between the Wars*' — the journal of a Thames, Medway and Coastal bargeman.

John Huggins founded a college at Northfleet in the 19th Century after having been refused permission to build in his native Sittingbourne. He chose this river-side site as his family traded along the Thames Estuary. He died in 1865 and was buried in Northfleet Churchyard. The buildings have since been demolished and a small chapel and replacement accommodation were constructed.

The Technical School with its statue of Queen Victoria (presented by George Arnold – an education pioneer). It was established as a Municipal Technical School around 1890, controlled by the local authority to provide 'instruction in Science, art and cookery to students of both sexes from the age of 11 upwards'. The fee was £1 per term or £1.10s should the pupil live outside the borough. Very soon after the opening the curriculum was expanded to cover many academic and technical subjects.

Fort Gardens (opposite East Terrace and Milton Place), surround New Tavern Fort built during 1779-80 and re-designed during 1868 and 1872. Nearby was Fort House the residence of the Commanding R. Engineer, then General Gordon, who assisted the poor and needy of Gravesend. In 1830 it was a private school and at one time housed the town clerk but was blown to pieces during the second world war. Today it is the site of a rose garden.

At the end of the 16th Century Robert Peverell was licensed to keep school and teach in Gravesend. In 1595 the corporation, as such, had a free school probably near the market place. The Free School was merged in 1830 with the National School. Many board schools were set up after the 1870 Acts, as well as several private schools including the Bronte School and Gads Hill Place at Higham. Here is the Modern School at Gravesend.

ROSHERVILLE GARDENS, MAIN ENTRANCE.

Extract from Crundens' *History of Gravesend:*—

1840 — At Rosherville, situated at the east end of the parish of Northfleet, adjoining the parish of Gravesend, Gardens of surpassing beauty have been formed; and a Pier in connexion with them, has been erected. Rosherville Gardens were entered by the south-west corner of Lansdowne Square. They were laid out by George Jones in a disused chalk pit lying between Crete Hill Road and London Road.

The pleasing gardens were often frequented by day trippers from London and included classical ornaments, terraces and even an archery course. At dusk the gardens were illuminated by hundreds of coloured lights, firework displays and 'fair' type performers. Over 20,000 people passed through the gardens in 1857 and by 1880 they reached their 'peak' in popularity.

The Rosherville Hotel with barely a room to let during 'Gravesend Yacht Week'. It was used as a hospital during the First World War and demolished in 1968 after having been converted into flats.

From the late 1880's the popularity of the gardens had begun to wane. They were closed in 1901 and only re-opened for the summer season in 1903 and each year until 1911. The archery lawn then became a football pitch. Part of the grounds were sold off to Henleys Cable Works in 1926 and the remainder followed in 1937 after a closing down fete, to become the A.E.I. Henley works.

St. Peter and St. Paul's Church at Milton dates back to the 14th century although it is thought to be on the site of a Saxon church. The fine tower contains a peal of eight bells, five of which were hung in the mid-seventeenth century. The clock was added in 1875. The organ installed in 1829 was re-built in 1887 and renovated in 1936. On the eastern wall can be seen the outline of either a very large window or a former chancel arch.

VIEW OF MILTON-NEXT-GRAVESEND, SHEWING BARRACKS IN FOREGROUND. No. 5039

Milton barracks were constructed in 1863 on land purchased from the South Western Railway Company in 1860. It was occupied by many different regiments and was the seasonal headquarters of troops undergoing military training at The Butts at nearby Shorne Mead. The barracks were closed in the early seventies.

'The Echo' public house proudly advertising the 'New London Brewery' faces the watering place at Echo Square. Nearby was 'Milton Court' known locally as 'Simpsons Folly' after William Simpson had moved from Rosherville because the entrance tower to the gardens invaded the privacy of his house. Further along was the site of an old coaching inn frequented by the London and Dover coaches, where the 'Prince of Orange' Inn now stands. Alongside here was once a cricket ground.

Cobham Wood and its Hall, the seat of the Earl of Darnley was a favourite place of Charles Dickens. He often walked from Gads Hill to Cobham Church and the park is mentioned in *Pickwick* as 'an open park, with an ancient hall, displaying the quaint and picturesque architecture of Elizabeth's time' and in the *Uncommercial Traveller*, 'Likewise we see great interest in going round by the park plantations, under the overhanging boughs . . . and through the wood until we came to the Keepers Lodge.'

The Gravesend or to be accurate the 'Thames and Medway Canal' has an interesting history. It was cut to enable barges (as seen above) to travel to the Thames from the Medway avoiding the dangerous and time-consuming route via the Grain Peninsula. An Act was passed in 1800 permitting the canal to be constructed from Higham to Strood via a tunnel. The Gravesend part was opened in 1824 but the Port of London refused to permit a lock to project into the river and so it was only usable at high tide.

Can you recognize anyone in this 1910 view of the Silver Prize Band?

Dartford

Originally the site of a ford crossing the River Darent recorded as Tarentefort in 1086, Darenteford in 1089 and other derivations until Dartfourde in 1610.

This early view shows a cycle shop by the side of the bridge at the foot of East Hill. This is the oldest part of Dartford and over the bridge is the parish church of the Holy Trinity. The tower is Norman and the chancel is 13th century and has a rebuilt nave dating from the early 14th century. The nearby priory was occupied by Dominican nuns, who were established there by Edward III in 1346. Wat Tyler's insurrection began at Dartford in 1381.

Bearing little resemblance to modern day Dartford this view shows the opposite side of the church. Horse traffic and pedestrian power were the order of the day but even in the early years of the century sign boards and advertising matter became an unsightly intrusion into an otherwise picturesque scene. An electric tram can be seen coming past the church whilst gas was still the main service of street and shop sign lighting.

Dartford had about 1,200 inhabitants in 1650, its importance was due to the fact that it was the chief corn market in North West Kent. Seymour in his survey of 1776 tells us that 'The Town is finely watered with good Springs, and full of Inns, for the Conveniency of Travellers. The Market which is Kept on Saturday, is much frequented by Corn-chandlers and Mealmen. The yearly Fair, on the second of August, is noted for horses and bullocks!'

The public library beside Central Park at Dartford was constructed in 1916 by T. E. Tiffin. This view shows the stone cupola over the entrance and the church (with its strangely positioned clock) in the background. The quietness of this scene would be rudely awakened by today's volume of traffic as it follows the 'Grand Prix' one-way system around the Arndale Centre and on towards London.

Papermaking and Engineering are the main industries of Dartford, both having originated in the town. Papermaking in 1607 when the first mill was built by Sir John Spielman and Engineering in 1590 with the first English rolling-mill for iron sheets. The Grammar School built mainly between 1862-1866 by A. W. Blomfield. Additions were made in 1873, 1883 and 1904-5. This early view shows pupils by the wall and the watering trough in the Street (West Hill).

The derivation of Greenhithe is 'grene hyo' or green landing place or landing place at a grassy spot which is underlined by the view above. Today however, Greenhithe is rather a different story with its industrial air, the cement works with its dust spreading all over the area. There are few buildings remaining of any interest save for the late 18th century bank. The church was constructed in the mid-nineteenth century near Cobham Terrace, a row of Italianate villas built ten years earlier.

Erith town centre was largely reconstructed in the late sixties with housing estates surrounding the centre stretching as far as 'Thamesmead' in the former barren and dark marshes of the Thames Estuary. This post World War I view of West Street with the tram will revive memories in the older residents of this Outer London sprawl.

Woolwich was long a centre for boatbuilding and several remains of Roman vessels have been found. The Naval Dockyard and Arsenal was established by Henry the Eighth; he built his war galleon 'Harry Grâce de Dieu' there, laying the foundation of the British Navy. Iron ships took over in the middle of the last century and building was transferred elsewhere. The buildings were then used as an arsenal, for the making of ordnance and ammunition.

According to Seymour's Survey, Crayford is fourteen miles from London, had anciently a ford over the River Cray, a little above its influx into the Thames, near which place a stone bridge has since been erected. The view above shows the bridge and old High Street. The Archbishops of Canterbury had possessions in the area and Archbishop Courtenay had a market here on Tuesday, '20 Richard II' and a Fair on the Nativity of the Virgin Mary four days after.

There has been a settlement here for over 2,000 years, and various finds have been unearthed including the Iron Age settlement at Ramsden in 1957 and a Mesolithic site at Well Hill. The Archbishop of Canterbury also held the Manor of Great Orpington and development has only been relatively recent. There is a Priory, a pre-reformation rectory house dating from 1270, now providing a local meeting place within its pleasant and relaxing gardens.

Chislehurst dates from Saxon times being recorded in a charter of King Edgar as 'Cyselhyrst' – meaning a wood on gravel. There are still wooded areas around Chislehurst today, namely the protected Common. The settlement was an appendage of Dartford and was in the excluded class of lands being omitted from the Domesday Book. The separation came in 1611 when Sir Thomas Walsingham bought the land. The Walsinghams attended at Flodden, and at the Cloth of Gold in 1424

On the west side of Chislehurst Common is Camden Park incorporating a golf course, the clubhouse is Camden Place built in 1609, by William Camden. The owners in the early nineteenth century were tragically murdered by their footman who was caught and hung at Penenden Heath near Maidstone. There are also the Chislehurst Caves, said to date from the Roman period and largely the remains of chalk mines. On the common near the parish church is a rare village cockpit prior to its prohibition in 1834.

Chislehurst's roads are a pleasing blend of the old and the new, with many fine houses standing amid trees and spacious gardens. The shopping centre is enhanced by the near-by Common with its ponds, whilst the shops of Royal Parade look onto a village sign today erected in 1953 to commemorate the present Queen's coronation. It shows Queen Elizabeth I knighting one of the Walsinghams and the residents of the Chisle-hurst above would have surely approved.

Farnborough is a village of some antiquity for St. Giles' Fair which was originally granted in 1220 is held every year. The second ancient custom is connected with the church. Four hundred years ago George Dalten of Tubbenden (the name of the street scene below) left a bequest that a Rush Sermon be preached each year and this is carried out on the nearest Sunday to St. Peter's Day. The church dates from the 16th century replacing an older building damaged by gales.

This exceedingly rural view of Woolwich Road, Belvedere, with the horse and trap, recorded in 1910 is remarkably scarce. Today this whole area is covered in housing estates best viewed from the railway line cutting its way through suburbia. Richard de Lucy laid the foundation stone of an Augustinian abbey in 1178 and this abbey called 'Lesnes' was suppressed by Wolsey in 1525 and the buildings razed. The site was excavated between 1909-1913 and the remains stand isolated in a grassy bank

Here the Cenotaph arouses juvenile interest whilst the most notable claim to fame of this village is the 'Red House' the home of William Morris. Research informs us that the house was designed by Phillip Webb following a trip to observe the medieval cathedrals along the banks of the River Seine in 1858. There were numerous interesting features including a minstrels gallery, a splendid ceiling, home made furniture and misplaced stained-glass windows.

Pesvner is correct in his conclusion that 'it takes a considerable effort, surrounded by a sea of suburban semi-detacheds, to remember that Morris and his friends, arriving from London at Abbey Wood Station, had three miles to drive through the North Kent Countryside before they reached his home in its orchard of apple and cherry trees'.

Richard Church describes Eltham as 'this little village lay in the heart of royal life, seething with activity, and the comings and goings of the great ones of the realm'. The Palace was a medieval foundation and one of the seats of the Royal Court. King Edward IV rebuilt the great Banqueting Hall of Eltham and it was the setting for many splendid occasions until it lost favour to Greenwich in the sixteenth century. This corner of the Court Yard and its quietness bear little relation to today's busy Eltham.

The tranquil setting of the card above seems worlds apart from the Bexley of today. The village street is choked with traffic and only the Tudor Mansion of Hall Place is worthy of inspection. It is reputed that the Black Prince stayed at the Mansion and a nearby public house is named after him. Once there was a white weatherboard mill on the Cray, but it was destroyed by fire some years ago and all that is left of the village is the tiny church strangled once again by the traffic.

A Corner of Old Bromley

Bromley, whilst remaining geographically within Kent, has been lost administratively to Greater London since 1963. This is another area of modern suburbia with the former villages now lost. The area has a long history for the Romans settled here and Iron Age settlements have been excavated at nearby Orpington and Keston. Beckenham, once a municipal borough in its own right, was described in an 18th century account as 'a town as delightful as it is salubrious'.

In 1866 Bromley was described as a small town on high ground commanding good views and with a rapid increase of fine residences. It had one railway station (Bromley South, opened in 1858), a post office, petty sessions, a new town hall, churches, a national school and a literary institute. Its property value was £28,565, it had 1,338 houses and a population, including the hamlet of Hayes, of 8,028. This had increased in 1965 to 69,910.

Bromley received its first charter in 1205 for a market and two annual fairs on St. James' Day and St. Blaise's Day. These were last held in 1862. During the 1930's the town centre was re-developed and the unusual dual-carriageway was constructed. During these alterations the house where H. G. Wells was born in 1866 (No. 47 High Street) was demolished and only a plaque on the store and the excellent collection of books in the library stand to his memory.

Several older buildings survive in Bromley, namely the Palace and the College. In 862 Ethelbert, King of Kent, granted land for the Manor of Bromley. It passed to the Bishops of Rochester in the 10th Century and was held by them until 1845. Shortly after the Conquest one of the bishops built the palace, which was rebuilt in 1775, later to become Stockwell College. Bromley College, however, was founded in 1666 to accommodate 40 widows of clergymen.

Hayes Village shown above before the encroachment from bustling Bromley denied its individuality. Here at Hayes Place, opposite the church, William Pitt the Elder and Younger lived – although the building was demolished in 1934. Alongside Hayes Common, Keston's Caesar's Well fitted out as a 'cold-bath' in the 18th century. Nearby is Caesar's Camp, a surviving relic of an ancient British encampment where coins, tiles and ancient remains have been discovered.

Rochester Cathedral.